Jennie Farley

My Grandmother Skating

For Angela -
thankyou for your
generous words!
with love
Jennie

Indigo Dreams Publishing

First Edition: My Grandmother Skating
First published in Great Britain in 2016 by:
Indigo Dreams Publishing
24 Forest Houses
Halwill
Beaworthy
EX21 5UU

www.indigodreams.co.uk

Jennie Farley has asserted her right under the Copyright, Designs and Patents Act 1988 to be identified as the author of this work.
©2016 Jennie Farley

ISBN 978-1-910834-23-7

British Library Cataloguing in Publication Data. A CIP record for this book can be obtained from the British Library.

This book is sold subject to the condition that it shall not, by way of trade or otherwise, be lent, re-sold, hired out, or otherwise circulated without the author's and publisher's prior consent in any form of binding or cover other than that in which it is published and without a similar condition including this condition being imposed on the subsequent purchaser.

Designed and typeset in Palatino Linotype by Indigo Dreams.
Cover design by Ronnie Goodyer at Indigo Dreams

Printed and bound in Great Britain by 4Edge Ltd
www.4edge.co.uk

Papers used by Indigo Dreams are recyclable products made from wood grown in sustainable forests following the guidance of the Forest Stewardship Council.

For my mother and father

Acknowledgements

Grateful thanks to my good friend and great poet, David Clarke, for his encouragement, patience and huge help with putting this collection together, and for our many stimulating chats. Acknowledgements due to the editors of those magazines and anthologies in which some of these poems have appeared, *New Welsh Review, Slow Dancer, Under the Radar, The Interpreter's House, Oxford Poetry, Lunar Poetry, Prole, The Cannon's Mouth, Dear World.* I would also like to express thanks to those who have given me the opportunity to share my work: Cheltenham Literature Festival; Cheltenham Everyman Theatre; Anna Saunders, Director of the Cheltenham Poetry Festival; Hilda Sheehan at the Swindon Poetry Festival; Angela France of *Buzzwords;* Rona Laycock at New Brewery Arts, Cirencester; Sharon Larkin and Roger Turner at *Poetry Cafe-Refreshed,* and to my poetry friends. Special thanks go to my publishers, Ronnie Goodyer and Dawn Bauling of Indigo Dreams Publishing; such a pleasure to work with!

Also by Jennie Farley

Jocasta's Song (Griffin Press, 2015)
Masks and Feathers (The Palms Studio, Cornwall, 2012)

CONTENTS

Horse: Mirror of Man 9
Maria and the Flying Saucer 10
Hollywood Nails 11
Cuttlefish 12
Snow Journeys 13
Streets 14
My Grandmother Skating 15
World's Edge 17
Sea Change 18
Pentire Point 19
Scarborough 20
Mister Peg and the Sunflower 21
Fur 22
Mischief 23
Dobbin 24
Mr Middleton 25
Californian Poppy 26
Games 27
Rosie Pigeon 28
Mandy in her Pink Swimsuit 29
Rosa's Dream 30
The Kiss 31
Purple Velvet 32
Watching the Sumo Wrestling 33
Pigeon 34
Wolf 35
Gone Girl 36
Karaoke 37
Parcour 38
Ride 39

Elvis Presley's Other Daughter	40
Feathers	41
Hedge of Thorns	43
Beast	44
Birds	45
Apples	46
Sheep	47
Glass	48
Hecate	49
Sleight of Hand	50
Silk	51
Alice	52
The Stopped Clock	53
Silver Horses	54
Willow Pattern	55
Buttons	56
What She Wants	57
Moth	58
Feeding the Hens	59
That Time of Evening	60

My Grandmother Skating

Tell all the Truth but tell it slant
Emily Dickinson

Horse: Mirror of Man
Lithograph from Anatomia del Cavallo c.1600

Stripped of hide and heart, packed muscles
pulled away to show a structure

ancient and strange as ivory.
Six-petalled stars circle the flayed creature

high-stepping among grasses, flowers,
stones, the sweeping tail tied with ribbons,

marked sections answering to the Zodiac,
a grid of prophecies. Picture this.

The artist in his studio, candle flame,
shadows pooling, flensing knives

steeped in blood, the stench.
A stoop-backed figure clenching

scalpel and graver cuts with mordant salts
the copper plate, reveals the arcane reality

of *the body of the horse,* the wonder of it:
beyond his vision the unreachable Soul

scattered as innumerable stars
sparking the firmament.

Maria and the Flying Saucer

Maria is waiting at the bus-stop
dazed by cow parsley and sun,
and the thought of all those pints she's pulled,
pies served, at *The Green Man*.

On her way through the churchyard
her heart soared. *Joy of Man's Desiring*.
The choir's throats became the throats of birds
and foliate heads roared in the undergrowth.

Sitting on a bench in the sun's crease,
she plucks the hem of her cheap summer skirt,
sniffs her warm brown arms.

She is waiting for a miracle.
The hour of the day
passes through her,
turning on the growth
of knowledge in her heart.

She recalls looking into a rainbow
through a garden spray,
seeing the moon's ghost
in the daytime sky.

The bus is late. Maria dreams:
she is wearing white lace gloves,
gardenias in her hair.

Is it the sun's heat that rouses her?
Or something dark, silvery and vast,
moving slowly into sight
    and dazzling...

Hollywood Nails

She's gone to get her nails done:
it always cheers her up.
A burlesque of gloss and glitter:
Alchemy, Rouge Noir, Rebel.
She spreads her hands
as if in supplication.

Soft fingers smooth
her scrubbed-raw thumbs.
A neat silver file
pares away domestic dross:
soapsuds, beer stains, nappies.

She drifts on lotus-scented clouds
amid the chirruping
of tiny Oriental birds.

Now, buffed and bright,
her fingertips take charge,
touching her life to light.
Swaying homeward
along the willow walk
proud in fine silks,
she unfurls
her gold-thread sleeves,
rasps her blood-red nails
along the birdcage bars,
hears her pet lark sing.

Cuttlefish

She dangled the baby over the balcony.
Who could do such a thing!
She'd tried beseeching, screaming;
tugged at his sleeve till it tore from his jacket.
She'd like to gouge blood from his stony face.
He never spoke, just turned,
and walked out the door.

Her belly swelled, she vomited:
she felt like rotting fruit, sticky and stinking.
She craved cuttlefish. She would go to the fish market
with bed-mussed hair, cigarette burns on her worn bathrobe.
There was something about fish, the stink of it, seaweed,
slime... She painted her nails vermillion, grew them long.
Ticked off the days. Her waters broke.

Back home on shore leave, cocky, suntanned,
swaggering along the familiar road:
he scarcely paused to wonder at the crowd
of women on the concourse, the upraised faces,
the figure on the balcony, the shawl-wrapped bundle.

Snow Journeys

All those journeys we used to make, our sleigh
(or grandfather's black Bentley) speeding
through the hushed and frozen night, that time
we fled S. Petersburg, the air heavy
with chypre and the scent of fur, warm plush
prickling our legs. The pale Empress (or
my grandmother) sat straight-backed. Her rings
smoked topaz fire across the glass, summoning forests
glittering with assassins and the threat of wolves.
Snuggled deep in winter dark, comforted by leather
and the green fizz of sherbet on the tongue,
I urged the pace. Our hastening tracks left
echoes of tiny bells, the dogs' breath furling back
across the glinting minarets, the city's glow
(or Market Square lamplit at closing time).

These were journeys I had to make,
across the table of the world,
away from the ordinariness of lives,
toward the long slow melt and miracles.

Streets
After a line by Philip Pullman

Beyond *the streets where the real and unreal
jostle* there is a ghost metropolis, a slippery
web of pavements where only the senses speak,
like the pure bellnote of a chorister's heartless hymn,
forest-musk brought in on a country boot,
the rough touch of memory, ingrained concrete walls,
smoke on the palate, the many tastes of snow.
There are whispers of winter at the violet hour
of dusk, muffled hoofbeats, carriage wheels,
a whiff of cardamom and fur, lamplit windows.
Loneliness beckons us to follow the line of trees
and out of town. At a posting-box a woman hovers,
letter in hand. Should she? We'll never know.
It's what we carry with us, our senses mingling
to make a jumbled sense of what this is. It's all we have.

My Grandmother Skating
i.m. Mary Elizabeth, my maternal grandmother.

That woman skating
against a winter sky,
her blades making

sure arcs on
the ice, alone
and concentrating only

on the moment
as she skates perfect circles,
is my grandmother.

Maybe it is
her sewing she thinks of,
on her way to Boston

to buy pearl buttons
and ribbon, or the fruit pie
she will bake

for Alfred's tea, the man
who years ahead
will be my grandfather.

As the huge sun fires
the horizon's dip and
her breath smokes white

banners on the frosted
air, she lifts wide
her skater's arms,

her gaze containing
fen, dyke, spire, then rising
to seek distances beyond the flatlands,

and gallantly strikes out, steel following steel, in ever widening perspectives.

World's Edge

So we have come to the world's edge
after all that driving through cabbage fields
and dykes, the flatlands of Lincolnshire,
the low wide sky. My mother beside me
recalling her childhood, the village
of Swineshead, Granny Craven's farm,
and the Brewsters, our ancestors, who left
to join the pilgrim ship those many years ago.

Soft Suffolk lanes led us to this coastal town
with houses colour-washed and quaint,
the half-timbered hotel standing
between reeded river and North Sea,
near a small white coastguard station.

At the close of this mellow gold October day
grey fog rolls in. With evening comes
a damp that mists our faces, the sea
is shrouded. We hear beyond the railings
the drag of shingle, farther out a foghorn's
moan. Unlocated ships, distant capes:
on that out-of-sight horizon past and
future meet. Like that once un-
discovered New England shore
the Rock of Ages awaits all pilgrims.

I turn from the sea, and steer mother
up the hotel steps into light and warmth,
and dinner waiting. Her present pilgrim voyage
is to the desserts trolley, and the big decision.
Sherry trifle? Or profiteroles with hot chocolate sauce?

Sea Change

Walking beside the sea is what people do,
with a happy dog, perhaps, or alone
gathering thoughts and stones and shells.

But I don't get that holiday feeling.
I see a vast continent of loneliness
you cannot begin to think about.

Ever-changing, treacherous:
today a blueness lulls you into wonder,
tomorrow the melancholy of deep sea mist.

Who knows what exists beneath, what secrets
lie buried in this dark grave of water. Old ships,
human bones churned to salt, strange creatures

known only to the deep. On the incoming
surf boys in slippery black turn into seals
as they dare the high wave's arc.

Barefoot on the shoreline, I hold
the sea-swell of terror close within
myself as I paddle in the wavelets' ripple.

Pentire Point
for Hannah

I heard that a woman had thrown herself
three hundred feet onto black rocks.
Hard to believe on a day like this.
Silver-glazed, blue, gorse budding gold,
the sand-scumbled grass smelling sweet
and warm. The promise of summer
should have vanquished
whatever demons troubled her,
the far-out horizon tethering sky
and ocean, the white gulls soaring.

I don't believe in ghosts. But from
below I hear the sea sigh to itself,
I see spume rise as a sweep of stairs,
at the top a woman poised to leap,
in her arms a bundle shawled in sea-mist.

Scarborough

At mealtimes grandmama
spits fiercely on her fingers, teasing
the corner of the linen tablecloth
to test for starch. She makes me
hold my knife and fork just so,
I can't cut the slippery pieces
of bleeding pink. She calls
the waiter and complains
about the gravy.

Sharing a bedroom with her
is like a nasty bedtime story.
Her loosened red hair fizzes
into mad corkscrews,
her nightie smells
of old biscuits
and Vicks Vaporub.
She mumbles in her sleep.

She won't let me play with
the donkeys on the beach.
I want to go home.
I want a supper of fish fingers
with *Blue Peter* on the telly.
She can read my ungrateful thoughts.
She smacks my bare legs, hard.
I pick up my doll and smash
her pot head on the hotel's posh hall floor.

Mister Peg and the Sunflower

The biggest peg from Mum's peg-bag,
inked-in eyes, nose, mouth. I give
the clues. The cousins search.

This is a game I invented
down at the allotments
when the cousins came to stay,

I wasn't allowed there on my own.
*Mister Peg is swinging
from a purple-speckled bell ...*

The cousins wander off to play
with bats and balls, real things,
leaving Mister Peg and me

alone among the foxgloves.
*Mister Peg meets a golden-haloed angel
standing tall above the bean rows.*

The angel shows me hidden places,
the nest of secrets beneath the rusting bench
where granddads sit chewing on baccy

and old urges, the marrow-growing feuds.
The angel tells me what goes on behind
the latched door of the tool shed.

Fur

Melanie has a new baby sister.
She hasn't got a name.
*Ooh*s and *aahs* and *isn't she sweet?*
I don't think so. I take a peek
at Mum's tummy every now and then.
She is wearing a camel-hair coat

Daddy bought for her from Jessops.
I wouldn't want a baby in my bedroom
sharing my dolls and chattering.
My dog Bouncer is all I want.
I don't mind his muddy paws
and stinky breath. We play ball
together in the garden,
I dress him up in my old cardies,
feed him pancakes and jam.

If there has to be a baby sister
tucked beneath Mum's new coat,
then I will make magic. I will dance
barefoot with Bouncer on the lawn,
chanting *abracadabras*...
When she pops out into the world
she'll be clad from top to toe in fur.

Mischief

Into the cupboard with Mister Fox.
He's red and whiskery, bold and sly –
and not quite a gentleman.
Prickles sparkle down my spine
as I feel a hard paw pat my knee.

I follow the wag of his white-tipped tail
through the back of the cupboard
to the open sea, across a swamp
of feathers, chewed-up bones,
doll's cracked heads and stolen sweets.
I tuck my frock into my knickers
as he turns to me with his foxy grin
and we dance the polka over the sands.

Dobbin

I am happy being the back legs of the horse,
it's snug and warm in here. The front is Susan.

My arms clasp Susan's waist, she steps out
boldly and I follow. One-step, two-step,

hop, and sway. Susan makes the horse-head
nod, open wide its big-tooth grin.

Clashing cymbals, flutes and drums herald
the Demon King, cheeky Buttons, the Sisters

with rubber-red mouths and floor-mop wigs.
We clomp on stage to shrieks and jeers.

Shadrach, Meshach, Abednego. My mantra
to protect me from the gymslip girls, from sticks

and stones, the fiery furnace. Don't they know
I am a flying horse with hooves of steel?

Mr Middleton

That smudge in the holly bush – it could be a bird,
but I know it is the ghost of Mr Middleton.
I know he's dead because the grown-ups *shush*
when I come into the room, because I missed

the grouchy nod at his front gate on my way
to school, because my gone-over ball hasn't
been chucked back. Found this morning in his chair
when Mrs Parker came. He'd finished his cocoa,

but not the crossword. At bedtime when my light's
turned off I can't stop thinking about Mr Middleton.
Will they take his teeth out, and will the tooth fairy come.
Will he keep his slippers on. The only dead person
I've seen is that thin pale man in a nappy, crying
tears of blood, who we pray to in church. Mr Middleton
won't smell any more of tobacco and cold gravy.
The holly bush his side of the garden won't get trimmed.

Californian Poppy

I would practice French kissing
with my teddy bear, then
I joined the gymslip girls

behind the games sheds after school.
We shared a slick of *Tangee,*
took turns at being Rock Hudson.

I kicked my right leg back
and up to flick my navy skirt,
leaned in for the kiss.

Our audience was the laughing sun.
One day I took a bottle of *Californian
Poppy* from Mum's dressing table,

pulled out the tiny rubber stopper,
dabbed each eager wrist.
Swooning, we sniffed a dream

of dusty freeways, brown hands,
cocktails with pink straws served
with tiny paper parasols and ice.

Games

Time to play dead, she says.
We lie down in a row beside

the tennis courts. We cross
our hands upon our chests.

The sky is brighter than blue,
hurting my eyes. I close them,

and in the afterglow see
what I most dread – angel wings,

a me-sized white coffin, a bunch
of lilies and my family weeping.

The others have got up and gone.
But I must stay here playing dead

beside the courts where the gymslip
girls are playing tennis forever.

Rosie Pigeon

Rosie Pigeon, Rosie Pigeon.
Up and down the street all day,
cooing, mumbling, pram wheels
grumbling. Us kids would taunt you,
call you names, dare each other to peek
beneath the hood. What did you keep
in that black pram? Dead rabbits,
chicken bones, a straw doll torn
to shreds? Beneath a fester
of curdled blankets comes a whiff
of fox, wool-mould, milk gone sour.

A bunched fist, a tin-sharp glare,
then off she goes, cooing mumbling,
pram wheels grumbling, trailing
some weird refrain, a lullaby, a dirge.

Rosie Pigeon, Rosie Pigeon. Tell me
what was it you kept hidden in your pram?

Mandy in her Pink Swimsuit

The sun is shining
on Mandy in her pink swimsuit
alone beside the swimming pool:
sounds of tennis in the summer air.
Soon the pool will be in shadow.
On the terrace grown-ups
in deckchairs sip *Frascati*.

Mandy, who can make herself invisible,
ponders on a ladybird
just landed on her wrist.
Why red? Why two black spots?
She is the ladybird. Now
she ponders on her hand,
the skeleton beneath, so clean,
so much more beautiful
than veined flesh through which
the blood goes travelling. *This season
bones will be worn outside the skin.*

And suddenly she is out there floating
amongst it all, trees, water, sky;
beyond herself, beyond strangeness.

Tomorrow Mandy will get up
really early in her pink swimsuit,
come down to the pool, and dive
straight as an arrow, into the blue
centre of the turning world,
and swim the new day into existence.

Rosa's Dream

Rosa is riding on an elephant,
sitting sideways on a purple-tasselled mat,
a lizard in her hair blinking one-eyed in the sun.
Rosa is wearing white lace gloves, her toenails
painted pink. With silken reins she guides
the elephant slow-footed through the jungle
of her sleep. The hanging curtains of her hair
hide day-thoughts bright and cruel as a lover's
farewell kiss, night-dreams rise up threatening
from the unseen forest floor.

The elephant kneels down. Rosa rests her head
upon the wide fold of the ears as she hears
the beat of leather wings, sudden shrieks
and throaty moans, the mocking laugh of monkeys,
hiss of serpents, all sounds melded into
a canopy of rope and webbing.

The lungs of the jungle are calling her to bed,
a strange lullaby, a slow cradling,
a cargo of dark dreams.

The Kiss
after Auguste Rodin

The way you hold me, the scoop
of your arm making tenderness
of stone, cradled in our shadow's grace.

Our enwrapped limbs are silk,
the slope of your spine a perfect curve.
I reach up to embrace your stooping

head, my marble lips yield soft
as I drink from the bowl of your mouth.
Once we were rock, our rapture shaped

by axe and chisel, blessed by light.
But the life, the breath, is ours. We
would have made love this way anyhow.

Purple Velvet

Hard men, my Yakuza brothers.
They chased you through the neon streets
of Ginza in their Lamborghini Diablo.
They dragged you from your *gentsuki*,
kneecapped you, spat venom
into your eyes.

The eldest drew his Tanto blade,
chopped off your left hand's
pinky tip, gift-boxed it
in purple velvet.

The avenging brothers wanted
to believe it had been rape.

For me it was *rapture*.

I wear your finger bone against my throat:
a token of defended honour.
A token of my love.

Watching the Sumo Wrestling

On a clear day
you can see Mount Fuji:
in the plains it is *sakura*,
cherry-blossom time.

Huge quilted Buddhas
with black hair pasted on:
they are warming up for a *basho*,
a pillow fight. Lovers
lunging at each other's arms
like bull elephants
and hugging. Snake eyes.
Soft seas. Thighs
like plums.

Here comes Big Buddha
padding by on his elephant.
Baby Buddha lies
giggling in his cot,
pulling the wings off butterflies.

Paper flowers. The bamboo parts:
a dark face.
The curtains close.

Do you remember
the sweet kiss of the knives,
and how we sliced shins like peaches
until the juices ran?

Pigeon
for Eley

There was this woman in love with a pigeon,
she had her head trepanned so the pigeon
could build a nest in the hollow of her skull.
You hear of people in love with trees,
the lean smooth trunk, the mossy clefts,
a ferny smell more stench than scent,
more animal. Horses too.
Great muscle-gods with sweating flanks,
power only just reined in, reminding me of those
uncles with hot eyes and uncle-trouser-smell
that brought up my teenage blushes.
I had a friend would sit for hours on the riverbank
swimmingly in love with the deep-river-gaze
of one particular trout. Trees, horses,
a lovelorn trout, a woman who had a pigeon
build a love-nest in her skull. The many kinds
of love and what people will do for the sake of it.
Self-immolation at the altar of an ever-loving God,
the gold-embroidered Cross, the wine, the wafer.
At the Ganges a widow hurls herself upon
her husband's funeral pyre, devotion, duty,
ritualised into the relentless call of suttee.
The chinkle-chankle terror of the stable boy
who blinded horses for love of them
Love, the cherished trust of friendship.
Love, the treacherous yearning, the call of blood
to blood, the mating game. True, and twisted.
The monster's cry: *All I ask is the possibility of love.*

Wolf

I remember suckling on sweetness
among a squirming furry jostle
of muzzles, paws and nippings.
Then I became a four-limbed thing
with waxy skin and scraps of hair.
I envied their pelts of silvery grey.

The day came when I lolloped off
on all-fours, helter-skelter,
dropping a trail of bloodspots
behind me on the snow.
I followed three raven feathers
to an ivy-shrouded door

opening onto mouldering silks,
veils and masks and wands.
I snatched a piece of bridal lace
to staunch my bleeding.
I hunkered down to lap at a pool
wreathed in leaves and mottled

by moonlight. A strange face, bone-pale
and bloodied, stared at me. A face
like the one I saw chalked above
the altar in the forest church, where
I was hunted down and brought
howling to this barren place.

Gone Girl

The girl was playing beside the brook,
singing, picking iris, hyacinth,
wild roses: then she was gone.

Her mother is guardian of the earth,
nurturer, bringer of seasons.
She covers wood and orchard
with her green quilt, smiling
golden light and warmth at harvest time.

Now she weeps as she gathers up
strewn blossoms, clasping
the sheaf corpse-like against her breast.

In her dreams she sees her daughter
cast with a sweep of shadow,
wandering among great black rocks,
singing brokenly, wanting flowers.

Cloaked in rags, like some wild bird,
the mother tears through town and field
waving her torch, grazing the world
with her grief. She invokes the tempest's
rage. Crops lie flattened, bones
of starved cattle await the ravens'
picking, the brook sheets with ice: all this

until her girl emerges from the dark,
her face pale as the first spring flower.

Karaoke

There's always three of them,
downing margaritas, loading the juke box,
performing karaoke as a three-girl troupe,
eyed up by every bloke on shore leave
leaning against the bar.

These three might be reclining
on a salt-sprayed rock in the old Aegean sea,
flicking their garlanded hair, bare arms
beckoning as they slink and croon
come-hither songs to passing mariners

Later in the bar there's one of them
that sits apart, quite still, holding her glass
as she holds your gaze, her storm-dark eyes
making you believe the unbelievable
about yourself. It is her voice alone
you hear, purple notes that twist your gut.

You could tie yourself to the mast
of your ship when her song calls
out to you, lest you be tempted
to let down anchor and set foot
upon the meadow-rock starred
with the bird-picked bones
of those sailors who succumbed.

You watch as slowly she sets down
her drink, slithers off the barstool,
takes a pack of smokes from between
her spangled breasts, moves towards the door.
There's no need for her to catch your eye.
Fingering the Rizlas in the back pocket
of your jeans, you follow her.

Parcour

Every leap is always the first, scaling
a landscape of cranes, towers, rusted
dockyard hulks. Don't look down.

A cold wind throbs in his mind's rigging
like the constant beat of gangsta rap
plundering the underpass. He shivers

in the sweat-shit shame of fear.
With the bravado of a one-night-stand
he stands poised on the rim, ready to tip

and turn a back-flip, or swing from
another's inked and muscled wrist.
One hundred metre drop. Time enough

to feel her fingers letting him loose
in the slipstream of his lust, as far
below police patrol the empty tracks

through willow herb, used needles,
empty cans, where once he lay with her
in safety, promising her the world.

Ride
after Lana del Rey

All I can say is it was what I wanted then,
warmed by the rush of Acapulco Gold,
dazzled by the glitter of despair.

I found myself drinking late into the night
in backroom bars. Killer heels. Crimson lips.
I wanted it rough and dirty, craving comfort

from the fumy sweat of strangers,
slick hands, tongues... believing
this would make my life a work of art:

a road movie, maybe, with me headlining the cast
of bikers in battered leathers, bandannas, clinging
to the backs of each in turn. I must confess

it was a crazy ride, racing the slippery highways
to the edge of danger, so that I almost welcomed
a swerving crash, an easy fall from that blighted paradise.

Elvis Presley's Other Daughter

You've no idea how long it took
for me to learn to stand this way,
the hip jutting, my hand thrusting

the pocket of my satin jumpsuit.
I've perfected the sneer. Everyone says
I am quite as pretty as you, my eyes

the same Hawaiian blue. Your Memphis
tomb soars in a sea of leaves. My mother
watched your funeral on TV. She wears

a slick of your hair close to her heart
and, lonesome, waits forever for your roses.
This is my story now. I dream

in marble light, shrugging my hip
as I stride soundless in my blue suede shoes
through empty halls. A single grace note

from a beat-up guitar sends echoes
rocking and rolling over the fallen leaves.

Feathers

It was his job
to brush the hair
fronding their hooves
like feathers.
He felt safe in the stable dark,
the warm herby smell
of horse dung and hay,
safe from the stares.
The circus freak.

In the ring
he'd crouch in the sawdust,
willing himself somewhere else:
a bird's cry hiding in a trumpet.

Drumroll and cymbals
sounded through holes in the wind.

High above him
hers was a magical act.
Crowned with bright feathers
her costume spangled the rigging
like stars. He would look up
and see her there, dreaming
her wonderful, dreaming the world.

And now he is up there (the circus freak)
tied to her by some terrible rope.
There is no safety net.

Cut the rope, and he'd go flying
over the world's rim.
The rope stays, his lifeblood
runs backwards.

He is up there
with her, poised on points of light.
The dissolving sky,
the falling would be soft
as the milk of angels
welcoming him into the dark.

Hedge of Thorns

My sixteenth birthday. I'm treated
like a slave. Up and down with trays,
and armfuls of wool for spinning.

She wants her cup of tea, she
needs her shawl. I'm so weary,
I could sleep for one hundred years.

I nod off at my wheel, a bead of red
pierces my fingertip, and the staircase
spirals my tumble into somewhere else.

Walkways silvered by sharp hoar frost,
and a woman tall as a tree grips my
hand as I pick the snowberries.

Now it seems like dusk, my pet goose
is leading me through a stony porch
webbed by candlelight into a memory

of rooms, hangings heavy with dust, carved
chairs that no one sits on. A trail of rusting
blood takes me down a passage heaped

with cinders to a narrow bed inside
a cupboard, where I lie rocking all night
long, dreaming of a boy with urgent hands.

One day my Prince will come. Hacking
through a millennium of binding roots,
to waken me with a kiss like a shiny key.

Beast

When he lumbers out from behind
the dark curtain into our living room,
visitors stare. They see huge crouched
shoulders roped with hair, bovine brow,
blubbery scowl: a monster in leather
armbands and thudding boots.

I don't need to close my eyes
to see a prince. He calls me *princess*
and my heart melts. His hands
are paws of gentleness, his kisses
sweet as plums. In the morning our bed
is rich with the scent of warm ripe musk.

Every night I pray that when I die
I will be lying in the blessing of his arms.

Birds
after The Pomps of the Subsoil by Leonora Carrington

I would slit my skin from sternum
to pubis, strip it from muscle, tendon,
bones, lay it on the ground for the birds
to peck at and bear their bloodied

shreddings to the sky. But I must
take up my paints. On a cobweb
spread of pastoral I will stretch out
something I have no words to say

in a language learned by listening
to the cosmos. If I could colour in
a peacock's cry it would be frosted fire;
angel-song, a sweep of bright plumage.

I straddle the easel, mix pigment, lift the brush.
Wait for my wounds to speak to me.

Apples
after Magritte

I remember his apple-breath
sharp amid the fruity tangs of autumn.

The apple fall that year was lush
with ripeness, in those bowler hat

and suited days when all at home seemed
safe, just before the world turned sour.

Seaside trips, summer hats, the parasol
he gave me: now gun smoke replaces

the memory of bonfires, roasting chestnuts
turned into cannonballs. I tiptoe along

the row of beds toward the flattened sheets
where his legs should be, his empty sleeve,

his eyes peeking out at me, bemused, from
behind the apple concealing what was his face.

Sheep

Marie Antoinette's flock of sheep is perfumed.
Every morning she trips barefoot across the dewy
grass, coiffed wig bobbing, brocaded silks
hooped up, pushing a small gilded wagon with wonky
wheels, heaped with ornate crystal flasks from her boudoir.

She calls each sheep by name: Marietta, Claudine,
Jacques... removes the gold stoppers one by one,
amber, tuberose and iris, anoints each fleecy head,
saving the costliest of all her scents for prancing
Jacques, her favourite. Baaings, bleatings,

a humping jostle, a haze of fruity musk
rises on the meadow air. She wrinkles
her nose, gives Jacques a hug, blows kisses.
A playful heart is dancing in her queen-cold breast.

Glass

I fear that I am made of glass, that I might shatter
at another's touch. Commoners and courtiers all
are shunned as I crouch in silent prayer

in my darkened turret room. Even the good Father
bringing bread and wine I urge to keep his distance,
and the ministering nurse with provender and physic.

A hermit-king, I emerge just once a day,
at cockcrow, while most men are still abed,
to perform a secret ritual to keep myself intact.

Thrice round the moat, my slippered feet tip-toeing
the dew-wet path, head down, mouth shielded
by my comforter (a small bed-blanket, sucked,

and warmly damp). While about these dawn
perambulations, three times I must pause:
once to stoop and pluck three ox-eye daisies,

twirl them to my nose; again to raise my fingers
to the scumbled stone and stroke that precious place
where time and weather have sketched the face

of my dead mother. Arriving at the castle gate
to meet my starting out, here for the third time
I must rest. I gather up my nightgown's fustian hem,

lean over the green-slimed wall and flutter my pale hand
at the still black water far below, a weed-framed mirror
from which a crazed and ghostly figure waves back at me.

Hecate

Sometimes I scare myself. When arsenic
bubbles blow from my mouth people flee,
when I up-raise my long-fingered palms
they beg for my blessing. By night

I travel the woods, snakes looped
around my wrists, my black polecat
at my side catching stars in his mouth.
I nod to the full bright moon and let loose

my balls of light to strike the knuckled stems
of corn so that they grow to twice their length,
then set to work scything circles of energy
and burn, seen at dawn as molten snow.

I have special gifts. I rearrange the strange
to create a lexicon of spells for good or evil,
comfort or revenge. But when I trespass
the hidden corners of men's hearts, I see

such pain and tears that no amount
of magical malarkey can heal. Even so,
I'm often found at the crossroads stone, waiting
for those lost souls and holding out my bag of tricks.

Sleight of Hand

You are dove.
Conjured from a flaring match
you fly to my shoulder, perch,
coo sweet nothings in my ear.

You are lion,
rampant, roaring
from a pennon sleeve
of scarlet silk.

When you are dove
I want to stroke
your soft white feathers,
cage you, pamper you,
until your frenzied flutter
breaks through the bars.

When you are lion
I want to fondle your mane
of rumpled fire as you lick honey
from my mouth, until you have
sucked out all my sweetness
and, sated, slouch away.

The man on the stage bows low,
shows empty sleeves. Raises his wand
to sketch a design of wings and pelt
across the falling curtain.

Silk

That louche shade suggests some secret
sin, the delicious scratch and tickle of lace.

I have to have them. I have to gratify some need
dangerous as lust. I've been wearing a shroud

of sadness, all-enveloping, opaque. Seen
through layers of gauze everywhere appears

far away and strange, sounds a distant hum.
I reach up. I don't snatch them, I let them

drop from the hanger onto my wrist,
slowly, like the Serpent's slither.

They're mine now. A deep twist of pleasure,
a frisson between my shoulder blades.

No one sees me at the lingerie rail. I hold
them tenderly in the ownership of fingers.

I crouch down, lift an ankle, raise my skirt,
and slide them on. Invincible, I step outside.

The day seems bigger, brighter now,
the shopping street more welcoming:

soft air upon my face, my hair, my hands,
my limbs seduced by the sly caress of silk.

Alice

Is it her tears? Or the sun
sparking rain-wet leaves?
A tracery of cobwebs,
splinters of bright.
She sees her crazed reflection
in a shattered looking glass.

Peacock feathers set the omens.
Live flowers, with the squashed faces
of tabby cats, jostle her daydreams
where she walks with the Red Queen.
Gnat, snap-dragonfly and bumblebee,
the rose, the lily, curtsey low.

That gentleman dressed in white paper
who gropes her mind is no more friend
than the shrill wind teasing out the World
beneath dead leaves, where claws of pain
are softening into feathers.

The Stopped Clock

The sound recordist turns on his machine
to capture silence. But the room has its own ideas.
Among the Meissen, the silver-framed
family photographs, the letters, there stands
a grandfather clock stopped at a certain hour.
The gentle hum of nothingness rises to
crescendo. The brocaded curtains quake
as at a sudden tug, the carpet trembles
to the tread of heavy boots, human cries
shudder in the architraves.

In the corner sits an old gentleman waiting
for the microphone. He knows these noises
all too well. But he will not tell.

Silver Horses

The afternoon is somewhere else.
I move slowly through a drowse
of sound. I steady myself
on ancient statues, unmoving
in this world of rippling opiate green.

Becalmed behind a pleasant
smile, I pat the bonnets of parked cars,
help myself to things in shops: nail polish,
silk scarves, a handbag. My voice
has become a Marlene Dietrich croon

as I embrace a lover I believe
I knew. When I close my eyes I see
a purple curtain alive with silver horses.
I am neither sad nor happy. If I weep
small tears then just for blighted love in TV soaps.

I chuckle at the antics of a neighbour's dog.
The hours of the day are measured.
I live for the moment when I lick
that sweet and sticky dewdrop
leaking from a black-edged petal.

Willow Pattern

The summer sky
is the exact blue
of that dress she wore,
I see it with my hard rinsed eye.
I see her features
in the clouds, constantly.

Her name means Beautiful Spring.
For me no Spring
will ever be beautiful again.

When a child dies
the text foreshortens.

Alone I sit
with needle fine,
embroidering
my Book of Days: rose-finches,
larks, my name Gold Flower,
stitching it, stitching it.

Silk sleeves cover my loss.
My heart is wintering
in a spice-dark cupboard.
Daily I take my tea
from fine bone china.
Beyond the bridge a lute sounds,
distantly.

My mind closes
as I creep the willow rim
of my grief
with bound feet, ceaselessly,
circling it, circling it,
travelling nowhere.

Buttons

She collects buttons. Why shouldn't she?
Some people collect china pigs, crocheted
cushions, cacti. So. She collects buttons.
From sewing-boxes, tins, musty coats
and frocks at Oxfam, occasionally from gutters.
The pockets of her cardi sag with button bounty,
her fingers twist with phantom 'doing up',
she'd never learnt the knack.

She is quite normal, apart from
her irrational fear of the colour yellow,
and that time she snatched a brass
button from a guardsman's tunic.
She wasn't arrested. She was taken
to a nearby bench by a kindly woman
who fed her humbugs and enquired
about her home life.

What She Wants

is to float in silks
over the rooftops.

To display herself to the world
below, a gorgeous cacophony
of sound and frenzy
in Chagall colours.

When the crematorium fire
has blazed her to glory
she can appear in whatever
guise she likes:

as a smoke-ghost
perching on the church steeple,
waving her legs, and shouting out
her lovers' names.

Moth
i.m. Shirley Bellwood, an artist and my great friend

And this is where we sat.
Two chairs, a corner of sunlight
hardening, as soon the chestnuts will,
in the green shade.

Beside the fossiled wall,
braiding lavender,
we shook out our scented aprons.

In the Victorian air-blue
we could hear echoes: other voices,
other days.

  A lead weight
falls faster than a feather,
  the feather slowed
     by air resistance.

White roses
in a late summer flush
crinolined the shrubbery.
Stone settled into folds of petals
while silence, listened-for, gathered
to itself the feline dusk.

A shadow pads the courtyard flags.
A paw. *My name is Moth.*

Feeding the Hens

Dusk, and she crosses the yard with her bucket,
the chickens cluck-clucking at her skirts:
and her mind turns inward, a river
running dark to its source.
She recalls her childhood, her sisters,
the high tree in the orchard, the swing,
swinging higher than clouds, higher
than the sky; her sisters brushing her hair
before bed – how it would spark!
This is one version of her life.

How the year her marriage failed
she went outside, knelt on the ground
and put a match to the wedding album,
dreams turning to ashes in her mouth.
Later, that Italian holiday, the burnished
light over the lake as he leaned on the oars,
smiling into her eyes. The taste of peaches.
Someone is playing Chopin in an empty room,
the window opens onto a summer garden.

Now her hands are age-speckled, there is frost
on her hair. Where has it all gone?
Twilight touches the yard, rain falls soft
as feathers, the hens come running.
She shakes out her apron, letting go
of the memories, letting them fly.

That Time of Evening

In the slant Sunday evening dusk
church bells peal, a scraping spade recalls
the glossy purple-black of plumes and horses,
iron wheels on cobbles.

Here comes the Preacher,
black book tucked beneath his arm.
His sermons are enough to unsettle the sun.
Tweed-capped lads bowl hoops, small girls
with hands in muffs trail boughs of holly.
Christmas card effects, but the Soul knows darker.

The Irishman with the lame white dog
loiters at the gate. Soon Old Leary
will come and touch the street to light.
The past is now. It might be
the ghastly clanging of tin cans
or a sweet bird singing.

Indigo Dreams Publishing Ltd
24, Forest Houses
Cookworthy Moor
Halwill
Beaworthy
Devon
EX21 5UU
www.indigodreams.co.